DEVOTIONS
FOR
CHURCH
SCHOOL
TEACHERS

RICHARD ANDERSEN

Publishing House
St. Louis

Concordia Publishing House, St. Louis, Missouri
Copyright © 1976 Concordia Publishing House
Manufactured in the United States of America

Library of Congress Cataloging in Publication Data
Andersen, Richard, 1931-
    Devotions for church school teachers.

    1. Sunday-school teachers—Prayer-books and devo-
tions—English. I. Title.
BV4596.S9A5   268'.4   76-1876
ISBN 0-570-03722-0

Soli Deo Gloria

Contents

From the Author   7
Alarm Clocks   9
In the Kindergarten of Faith   10
Called, Not Cornered   11
It's Been a Long Day   12
Sunday School All Week Long   14
I Pledge Allegiance   15
Speed Reading or *Need* Reading?   16
Songs That Shimmer   18
Chalk Power   19
Thesis on Thought   21
Between God and Ginott   22
Never Too Old to Learn   23
The Sunday PTA   25
Self-Examination   26
Object Lessons   27
Diploma to Discipleship   29
Extracurricular Activities   30
Between Parson and Guile   31
A Schoolhouse of Trees   33
Imaginative Evangelism   34
Child Talk   36
Popcorn Paraments   37
Too Many Hats?   38
Professionalism   40
Vacations   41
School Cheer   42
Detention   43
The Big Game   45
BMOC   46

From the Author . . .

The term "Christian education" covers a multitude of tasks. Learning is ever about us, and the Christian rejoices in teaching that gives meaning and delight to all there is to know.

The church or Sunday school —that age-old arena for teaching little children who are eager for the experience, adolescents who are easily distracted, mind-expanding teens, young adults with a world to tame, and adults who want to burrow more deeply in Scripture or climb much, much higher in social concerns—is a kaleidoscope of information, teaching devices, and opportunities. It is also a realm that can promise more in the name of Christ and deliver *far* more in the power of the Spirit.

Some seem to think it's time to junk the church school. Others find it a continuing challenge that they eagerly meet. If someone aims at defeat, he will get it even before the white flag is flown. If someone sees the goal as lives deepened and enriched and eternally won for Christ, then his or her sights are high enough and resources are ample.

Begin with prayer.

You're never too old to learn that the way to an enriched teaching career (in a Sunday school room or a secular or parochial classroom) is a dynamic prayer life, one that fairly explodes with gladness, that excitedly shares with the Master Teacher all the objectives as well as all the objections. Listen, then, as He responds with power-renewing might, with splendid holy love, with abundant forgiveness, with perspective and purpose and promise.

Education in all its varied dimensions is more than a grand adventure; it is a holy pilgrimage. When Christian instructors and Christian youths yield themselves to the power of the Triune God, marvelous things happen. Growth occurs. Not just outside, but within. One can almost feel the soul surging upward. But unlike psychedelic expansion, the soul expands for the assurance of the individual and for sharing with others.

May your adventure in the realm of teaching be more than books and papers, but truly Christian education! May you leap forward spiritually to tell the world that Christ lives within you! May you never fail to learn each lesson the day affords. But most of all, may you know that despite defeat, discouragement, trial and temptation, His victory is yours to delight in now and forever.

And it's possible; for you're never too old to learn!

Alarm Clocks

So wake up, and strengthen what you still have, before it dies
completely.
Rev. 3:3

It was a wild shriek in the ebony shadows of early morning,
enough to startle me, but insufficient to trumpet me to attention. I
had heard it too often before and met its scream with a wearied
groan each time. There was no "This is the day which the Lord has
made; let us rejoice and be glad in it" in that desperate scramble for
another five minutes in the sack. There was instead a slow, gradual
unfolding of my limbs and an even slower opening of my eyes to
behold the day that had arrived. Dawn was bursting to let its light
flood my room and my life.

And then it registered! The piercing call of the alarm clock was
my crowing rooster. Like Peter I had heard its warning before and
yielded to the easy denial, but not so this day. This was a new
opportunity to triumph over yesterday's mistakes.

This was a new day to check my caustic tongue. This was a new
day to fulfill my hopes for usefulness to God and men, to the
Sunday school and its many enrolled families. This was a brand
new dawn, with hours to be emptied of purposelessness and filled
with Christian service joyfully given.

This was another chance to flex the muscles of faith in Indian
wrestling with the impulse to set aside morality another day, to
scurry after every potential buck without caring how it's gotten, to
avoid responsibilities. I'm ready to use what God has given me to
do what God wants of me in order that He may be praised. I'm
ready, but Triumphant Spirit, prod me to do it.

It's routine, this daily ringing of the alarm, yet each new day is
another blank page in the accountant's register, a page to be filled
and balanced. Like bells calling classes to order, there is a new

opportunity to begin afresh the scholarly work that honors God. Success is not tallied in figures only; it's summed up in the satisfaction that comes from allowing God's day to be ordered by Him as we sensitively calculate His will for us.

Alarms and church bells awaken us to bright hopes and exciting challenges!

Let that ring echo within our souls all day to keep alive and strengthen what Christ has given us!

In the Kindergarten of Faith

Truly, I say to you, unless you turn and become like children, you will never enter the kingdom of heaven.
Matt. 18:3

The sophistication education creates can be more impenetrable than the Berlin Wall or the gate at Fort Knox. But education is a continually humbling experience for those who pursue it honestly; for the farther they travel along the road to knowledge, the greater the distance to their destination.

When Jesus was asked, "Who is the greatest in the kingdom of heaven?" He did not hesitate to single out a youngster as the object lesson. The faithful are called to the humility of a little child and to be as open to learning as children are, as trusting of Him as only children can be. In short, Jesus invites us all to continue in the kindergarten of faith, always receptive to truths He alone imparts, ready to confront every question with the certainty that in Him is the answer.

Surely that does not imply perpetuating ignorance. It means developing an awareness that the Triune God is at the center of all knowledge and that He gives meaning to everything. With the cross at the heart of Christian education, the ripples that radiate from it reach every shore of learning, for Christianity does not constrict knowledge but encourages it.

John Milton has told us that "the end of all learning is to know God, and out of that knowledge to love and imitate Him." Another Englishman has rightly said that "knowledge is but folly unless it is guided by grace."

Where but in the kindergarten of Christian faith can learning be so exciting, exacting, and enjoyable? Become, then, like children!

Called, Not Cornered

As the truth of Christ is in me, this boast of mine shall not be silenced.
2 Cor. 11:10

H. L. Mencken defined Sunday school as "a prison in which children do penance for the evil consciences of their parents." Unfortunately, many staff members have taken Mencken seriously and adopted the definition as their own. Somehow, they believe their willingness to join the Sunday school staff is next to martyrdom on a foreign field. They feel cornered. The more they get involved, the more depressed they become.

"Discipline can't be maintained."

"The curriculum is incomplete."

"The superintendent doesn't like me."

"I have too many responsibilities to really give preparation my all."

Arguments are offered and excuses provided, but the prison such a person finds himself in is not the Sunday school, the parish, or Christian education. It's the jail of penance; it's the motivationless pokey of guilt.

But Sunday school staffs are not to be concerned by either the board of parish education or their own consciences. If the truth of Jesus Christ has registered firmly within, then whatever obstacles there are to effective teaching become challenges that make for adventures, not crosses that make for adversity.

St. Paul boasted his way across Asia Minor and Southern Europe precisely because the truth of Christ in him was so effervescent that it bubbled into every relationship. He could not meet people without it inflating the association far above what others might expect. And they, too, caught his sparkling enthusiasm and shared the truth of Christ gladly with others.

To be a teacher of children is a high calling. To be a Christian teacher of youngsters enrolled in a program specifically aimed at cultivating their knowledge of the Bible and their receptivity to God's love is the loftiest calling of all.

Such honored instructors will honor Christ and their students only when the truth of Jesus will not allow them to be silenced or complain but only to boast of His love and His lordship.

Such instructors are truly called—called by God *as well as* the board of parish education.

It's Been a Long Day

And Jesus, tired out by the trip, sat down by the well.
John 4:6

I'm exhausted, Lord. Sundays are days of labor, loving labor in worship and Sunday school, youth work, and congregational activities.

You knew what it was like to be tired. I remember when You fell asleep in the boat as it crossed the indigo waters of the Sea of

Galilee; You were not even disturbed by the churning of the stormy lake. You were weary.

You were not so weary that You failed to answer the pleas of the disciples who were frightened by the lashing waves, nor were You so tired that you ignored the Samaritan woman drawing water at Jacob's Well. Was this the inspiration for St. Paul's admonition: "So let us not become tired of doing good; for if we do not give up, the time will come when we will reap the harvest" (Gal. 6:9)? And, of, "But you, brothers, must not get tired of doing good" (2 Thess. 3:13)? It must have been this unwillingness to yield to weariness that prompted the writer to the Hebrews to say, "Think of what He went through, how He put up with so much hatred from sinful men! So do not let yourselves become discouraged and give up" (12:3).

It's been a long day and my body aches from it, but I'm thankful, Lord. You gave me a body that absorbs the punishments of the day and is refreshed by a night's rest. You've given me a life that is renewed by Word and Sacraments; the old weary sins are peeled away for a brand new day. You've given me an existence in which I may hope and dream and see visions of possibilities. Every muscle pain, every ache from my big toe to my balding pate sings its thanksgiving for the ending day, as well as the beginning of tomorrow.

As I rest, I reflect on what was and what might have been. In my reverie I plan for new tomorrows in which I can grow weary with the pleasure of teaching the Gospel.

When I'm tired, my patience is in scant supply. After a busy day I don't have much energy to still storms raging around me, until I remember your response to those who bothered You. And even the children get to me, until I recall how You told the disciples: "Let the children come to Me" despite Your own weariness. Exhausted as I am, Lord, Your example renews me. It's been a long, but happy day.

Sunday School All Week Long

Train up a child in the way he should go, and when he is old he will not depart from it.
Prov. 22:6

Train yourself in godliness; for while bodily training is of some value, godliness is of value in every way, as it holds promise for the present life and also for the life to come.
1 Tim. 4:7-8

Teach what befits sound doctrine.
Titus 2:1

What about modern education? Is it Sunday school all week long?

The answer is "yes," if the dedicated Christian faculty found in Sunday schools is duplicated in the weekday school and the objective of teaching and reaching students for Christ is definitely there.

But the answer is also "no." In day schools, whether Christian, public, or private, the same basic curriculum demanded by the states is taught. The only difference is that Christ is given the place of honor by some, while others exclude Him, ignore Him, or "tone down" their teaching to avoid conflict.

We can still claim, however, that the Sunday school and the public school are colleagues in mission. They are complementary and share the mutual ministry of teaching students important truths and building generations for their future roles.

Hurrah for the Sunday school! Some have questioned its worth. Perhaps it can be drastically improved, but that's a matter of technique not purpose.

Hurrah for the Christian school! Without federal money it

succeeds in doing a superlative, well-rounded, cross-focused teaching job.

Hurrah for the public schools! Martin Luther had a hand in the birth of public education. Where overt witness is forbidden, Christians still are making their presence known by their winsome personalities, substantive counsel, and wise instruction. Christian students who have a good spiritual foundation from home are capable of discovering the truth and being a bit of leaven in the lump also.

Many youngsters have their first taste of school in Sunday school, and it's the pleasure of that experience that gives them a good start in public or day schools. When you're growing in Christ, the quest for more knowledge of Him and His Word goes beyond one hour a week.

I Pledge Allegiance

First of all, then, I urge that supplications, prayers, intercessions, and thanksgivings be made for all men, for kings and all who are in high positions, that we may lead a quiet and peaceable life, godly and respectful in every way. This is good, and it is acceptable in the sight of God our Savior.
1 Tim. 2:1-3

It was popular sport only a short time ago to disdain patriotism. The pledge to the flag was halfheartedly made, if at all, in many schoolrooms and assemblies. But that pledge, as brief as it is, still conveys the passionate prayer, the confident hope of every citizen who loves his country. I have often been moved to tears as Scouts led groups in the pledge, as veterans called crowds to attention, as school children invited their classes, "Ready, begin."

To honor nation and government is not to make idols of them, but to respect the orderly means by which God operates among men. "Government is instituted, not in order to seek its own profit at the expense of its subjects and to exercise its self-will on them," said Martin Luther, "but in order to provide for the best interest of its subjects."

How do we cultivate future leaders for our nation and the world, if we do not teach them loyalty to God and country? How do we inspire the best youth to aspire to high office if we take from them the fundamental supports of the pledge, national songs, and prayer for leadership in all levels of government?

It is for church school teacher and student alike to demand the best from each other that the nation might thrive. We pledge allegiance to our country most zealously when we equip each other with values that are founded upon a strong Christian faith and when we challenge one another and those in authority to fulfill their oaths as stalwarts of Biblical conviction.

To do less is to undermine our system, to cut short our democracy, and to invite tyrants to rule. More to be feared than overt patriotism is a people who don't care. Christian students and teachers afford the single best guard against such a tragedy befalling our land.

Speed Reading or Need Reading

All scripture is inspired by God and profitable for teaching, for reproof, for correction, and for training in righteousness, that the man of God may be complete, equipped for every good work.
2 Tim. 3:16-17

As commendable as is the ability to read rapidly and comprehend thoroughly, there is another ingredient well worth considering as even more important: the subject matter. An overemphasis on technique without attention to the kind of material read surely ignores a vital factor. There's more to the art than speed reading. It's called *need* reading.

Those involved in the interpersonal relationships of a church school, as students or members of the faculty, should study information that will help them smooth the wrinkles out of those relationships. God's Word provides abundant help. It is a spiritual book, the Bible, yet it is also a very pragmatic tool, enabling its readers to better cultivate their own gifts. In short, the Bible is a detailed course in successful living.

Study David, for instance, Peter or Paul, Abraham or Jacob, Mary Magdalene or Martha, and you will discover not only their gifts and assets, but the debits within their personalities. From them we learn invaluable lessons, lessons we need to apply in life. From them we gain inspiration and hope, knowing that even the strongest in faith possessed immense, but forgivable flaws.

Discouragement comes easily to church school teachers and learners alike; thus it is well to cultivate the Bible's positive spirit. The most necessary lesson of all, of course, is that God loves us, that His care is constant, and His power is readily available to enable believers to further His kingdom. This is not a lesson to be read too rapidly, but something to be absorbed, accepted, and acclaimed. The "complete" person, more than the "compleat angler," is God's good goal.

What you need is to read more of the Bible and *practice* what it teaches. But don't rush. This is a "slow zone."

Songs That Shimmer

O sing to the Lord a new song, for he has done marvelous things!
Psalm 98:1

Music is a matter of taste, they say, and my taste runs afield from much that vibrates from radio stations and stereo sets. But even then I catch my toes beginning to move with popular rhythms and my head nodding with their sounds.

The stately old chorales of the Christian faith are filled with beauty and immense meaning, but it is surprising how much faster youngsters respond to the words and music of contemporary songs. A guitar was once considered a rather unsophisticated instrument, but teenagers have acclaimed it as the national music maker. David's stringed instrument may have been different, but it was surely similar in being portable and popular. And the songs of the youth are no different in spiritual fervor than those of Havergal, Bach, or Wesley.

Their songs today shimmer with clapping and shouts of praise. The lyrics may speak today's jargon; but the old, old truth of Christ rings clear.

"Come to the Waters" is a song that flows with quiet joy. "Pass It On" encourages a happy witness. "Love, Love, Love" is today's "Jesus Loves Me." "Put Your Hand in the Hand of the Man Who Stills the Water" counsels wisely the errant soul. "We Are One in the Spirit" and "Sons of God, Hear His Holy Word" are becoming old standards in the folk mass. Refreshingly, the breeze that stirs new music stirs hearts as well.

A board of a major denomination met around a campfire in the cool stillness of a summery night in South Dakota's Black Hills. Youth from a nearby Bible camp led the singing. They sang the light and lilting tunes of Christian camp songs and the happy, bright folk music of today learned in Sunday school. Gradually the circle widened. Campers near the stream to the south joined the group. They were Christians from another state. A young couple had been strolling along the path that led to the State Game Lodge and were captivated by the singing. A group of youngsters, mostly Indians, who were involved in a special training program asked if they could participate. They brought their drum and kept rhythm with the songs, and they chanted an age-old song of their ancestors, but they also caught the flavor of the new songs they heard being sung.

These were songs that shimmered in the awesome majesty of that verdant retreat, and they were today's Sunday school songs that tell the world of the marvelous things of God.

If you're beginning to tire of the same old thing, take the Psalmist's advice and "sing to the Lord a new song, for He *has* done marvelous things" worth singing about.

Chalk Power

Jesus bent down and wrote with his finger on the ground. And as they continued to ask him, he stood up and said to them, "Let him who is without sin among you be the first to throw a stone at her."
John 8:6-7

Of all the teaching devices known to man, universally the most popular is the chalkboard. The remotest teaching stations on earth boast at least one such device. Overhead projectors are the modern, updated versions. Jesus had only the dust and His finger, but He used both to good advantage.

The event concerned a "woman who had been caught in adultery." The Mosaic law judged such persons guilty, and the cruel form of capital punishment known as "stoning" was considered fit for them. Jesus knew that her tormentors were testing Him; thus He sought to outwit them and did so. She was to be stoned by those *without* sin. Quietly He bent downward, and began anew to draw in the dust. In but a moment, He and the woman were alone.

"Woman, where are they? Has no one condemned you?" asked the Savior.

"No one, Lord," was her simple reply.

"Neither do I condemn you; go, and do not sin again."

He worked at His primitive "chalkboard" the formula that love alone dictates. Forgiveness, the practical application of love, was the only answer to her need and the dilemma imposed upon the Savior. Jesus did not condemn people, but He rejected their sinful acts. So He dealt with the Pharisees, Matthew, Zacchaeus, and Mary Magdalene as well as the adulterous woman.

At the chalkboards of our classrooms many arithmetic formulas are charted, many historical facts recorded, and many parts of speech defined, but nowhere can a more important truth be taught than the one imparted at the Mount of Olives: Love requires understanding; understanding demands forgiveness, and forgiveness implies a new resolve to "sin no more." Jesus' chalk-talk in the dust reminds us that His love is without end and His forgiveness unlimited. That's chalk power worth practicing by every Christian.

Thesis on Thought

Brethern, do not be children in your thinking; be babes in evil, but
in thinking be mature.
1 Cor. 14:20

Paul was an educated man. His faith was intellectually sound
as well as spiritually grounded. When he urges people to be mature
in thought, he is not suggesting they should base their faith on
reason. Even the child is capable of serious thought, but the mature
man can grapple with profound reasoning on a higher plane.

"Thinking is the hardest work there is, which is the probable
reason why so few engage in it," stated Henry Ford.

"Living truth is that alone which has its origin in thinking.
Just as a tree bears year after year the same fruit and yet fruit which
is each year new, so must all permanently valuable ideas be
continually born again in thought," observed Albert Schweitzer.

A Swiss educator, Johann Pestalozzi, focused on this idea:
"Thinking leads man to knowledge. He may see and hear, and read
and learn whatever he pleases, and as much as he pleases; he will
never know anything of it, except that which he has thought over,
that which by thinking he has made the property of his own mind.
Is it then saying too much if I say that man, by thinking only,
becomes truly man? Take away thought from man's life, and what
remains?"

There is so much for the intellect to consider that to put it on
perpetual vacation is tantamount to adopting the form and habits
of human beings, but the brainpower of lower primates. Within
the classroom of the Sunday school there is more intellectual
energy available than any institution has dared to use, yet such
gifts of God must not, like the soil, lie fallow for a season.

Stimulate thinking; motivate learning; encourage intellectual examination, and with it feed man's soul the truths of the Kingdom. Watch the church of Jesus Christ marshal the forces to breathe genuine love into a world dying from hate. Teachers and students, think! Think on Christ and His gospel and energize the world!

Between God and Ginott

What man of you, if his son asks him for bread, will give him a stone? Or if he asks for a fish, will give him a serpent? If you then, who are evil, know how to give good gifts to your children, how much more will your Father who is in heaven give good things to those who ask him! So whatever you wish that men would do to you, do so to them; for this is the law and the prophets.
Matt. 7:9-12

The late Haim Ginott taught America and the world how to talk to children. His best-selling books are found on many shelves across the land and have been tremendously helpful to parents and educators alike.

One of his concepts concerns "congruent communication," the means by which adults address the situations involving children rather than attacking the child's character or personality.

Jesus shows us the Biblical approach, which is not far from Ginott's. Children who request food of their parents should not be given rocks, but this is what's done when thoughtlessly we hand them insults rather than solutions.

Every now and then I'm asked to "talk" to a misbehaving youngster. The teacher gives me a quick rundown of the problem, and then the student and I spend some time together discussing both the teacher's charges and his own interpretation. I have learned that pastors must support their staffs, but that means studying the problem rather than attacking the student's character or lack of it. Similarly, a pastor or superintendent cannot ignore the student's own views, but must hear them out.

A student with a personality problem, who had little to do with the church despite his enrollment in a Christian school, was brought to me for consultation. I told him how pleased I had been with something he did a few days before. In a chapel service the faculty had worked very hard to put across the idea of "friendship" as something Christians work at. There had been some incidents that made the chapel topic worth the attention of all. That night the student I was to discipline had not left school, staying instead with a friendless youth who was waiting for his family to come. The student was handing bread to a friend who asked for it, and I was not about to hand him a stone.

Never Too Old to Learn

Wisdom is with the aged, and understanding in length of days.
Job 12:12

O God, from my youth thou hast taught me, and I still proclaim thy wondrous deeds. So even to old age and gray hairs . . .
Psalms 71:17-18a

If anyone already believe it, the American Association of Retired People will change his or her mind. In their publications and through their program they indicate with one example after another that continued education despite advanced years is far superior to taking to one's rocker until death comes.

There is the other perspective also. Children are never too young to learn something if they are normal and healthy. A tiny infant quickly begins to learn from its environment.

It is possible, unfortunately, to *refuse* to learn. Sometimes we say we have a "mental block" or complain, "It doesn't make sense." The genuine student is the one who recognizes these dodges for what they are and plows right on through them. The object is to learn.

I once had to substitute for an instructor in a day school. He had become suddenly ill. He had left no directives, and I could not find his lesson-plan book. It was an especially difficult class with a serious deportment problem. Quickly I assigned them the next chapter and a set number of problems in the mathematics text. I told them it was to be a period of challenge, since no instructions would be given, and they were to reason the problems as best they could.

Many gave up before opening their books. Several took the challenge as a great commission and zealously pursued the answers. They tried a variety of ways to make the problems work out correctly. Others groaned. One became very upset without even reading the text and sulked. Although none of the students got every detail of the complicated problems correct, several put so much into them that I was amazed. They *felt* as if they had succeeded. The feeling of success is not to be ignored.

We're never too old to learn, whether we're 5 or 105, but that implies something else about a person. When one looks on knowledge as buried gold that merely needs to be mined, one is not afraid of sweat. Grime is no bother, for something awaits that will make it worthwhile. And so it is for all who persist. God's unlimited gold mine is knowledge. Keep searching! It's to be found in the Sunday school room too!

The Sunday PTA

And we exhort you, brethren, admonish the idle, encourage the
fainthearted, help the weak, be patient with them all.
1 Thess. 5:14

*P*atience *T*o *A*ll is the PTA of the Sunday school.

*P*ractice *T*he *A*rt is the injunction of Scripture.

*P*raise *T*he *A*lmighty is the PTA of the Christian who knows
that "love is patient and kind," for he has experienced it and
applied it.

There is undoubtedly a time for impatience, but not until its
positive counterpart is steadfastly tried.

A mother was told her baby had cerebral palsy and would never
learn to walk or talk. It was a painful announcement, but she was
not lacking in courage or faith. She spent endless hours teaching
the baby to crawl for its bottle, and with every small victory she was
spiritually revived and maternally inspired.

Paul Scott could have been hospitalized and allowed to
vegetate, but instead a patient, determined mother made him a
walking miracle. His walk is jerky, but his feet are sure enough that
he has even learned tap dancing. He plays a trumpet, types, draws,
studies, and does everything with but a few exceptions that other
children do. He is personable, and the family is constantly praising
God for the miracle of Paul. Paul has taught his classmates the
meaning of patience also, a Christian patience that is structured on
faith in the Savior and love for all.

That's Paul's own PTA—*P*aul *T*eaches *A*gape—for in him it is
seen that "love *is patient and kind.*"

Paul's parents were not just unique, as someone has suggested.
They were faithful to God and His promises.

In the Sunday school such faith gets its start and nurture, but it has to mature to the extent that it can dare to Please The Almighty by a faith that looks beyond the superficial to the reality of the might and love of God.

It can't be just a Sunday PTA or even just a Sunday school PTA.

It has to be incorporated into life and become a part of every day.

Practice The Art with your class and watch them Praise The Almighty because you have given Christian Patience To All.

Self-Examination

Examine yourselves to see whether you are holding to your faith.
Test yourselves. Do you not realize that Jesus Christ is in you?—
unless indeed you fail to meet the test!
2 Cor. 13:5

Suppose church schools and Sunday schools started giving exams in earnest? It might prove a lot of things, and most would cringe with the thought of how negative such a practice might become. One might argue that children would never return if they were *threatened* with tests.

I'm never quite sure who dreads examinations more: the students or the staff. A good examination is work to prepare, just as it requires real effort to be passed. Yet the teacher is probably the one who gets short shrift, since the exams must be read to be graded. The pain is in discovering how the questions were misunderstood, the lessons misinterpreted, and the discussions misrepresented.

Examinations are necessary, even if they are a pain, and dangerous, as alleged, to give in Sunday school.

Wrote C. C. Colton, "Examinations are formidable even to the best prepared, for the greatest fool may ask more than the wisest man can answer." And that can be reversed.

That's why Paul advised the Corinthians to participate in self-examinations to determine the soundness of their faith. They alone determined the score. If, however, Christ's presence within life is recognized, enjoyed, and shared, then even personal examination need not be feared.

In one way or another all of us are preparing for the greatest final exam mankind knows. If we fail to apply faith in Christ to life, the danger is that we shall not be prepared to meet death with the certainty He alone conveys. The outcome could be tragic and unnecessary.

Thanks be to God, however, that He has sent His Holy Spirit to constantly "call, gather, enlighten, and sanctify" us so that we may be fully prepared for eternity's finals.

You cannot afford not to prepare your students for such a self-examination.

Object Lessons

Let not many of you become teachers, my brethren, for you know that we who teach shall be judged with greater strictness. For we all make many mistakes, and if any one makes no mistakes in what he says he is a perfect man, able to bridle the whole body also.
James 3:1-2

James is right. Teaching is serious business, holy and demanding. It is because of the wondrous grace of God that we dare teach anything, and it is because we are assured of the Spirit's presence that we meet success rather than defeat.

It is not always what we *say* that instructs our students. Many times our actions provide lessons they learn better. Often it is our out-of-the-teaching-role attitudes and language that leave the most lasting impression.

When I first began teaching in the Sunday school, the superintendent informed me there were two rules that he always wanted me to remember:

1. Teach each class as if it would be the only time I would ever be able to share the love of Jesus with those students.
2. Remember that my example roared while my instruction only squeaked.

He was suggesting that if I became delinquent in my worship habits, negligent of attending the Sacrament, or forgetful of such Christian characteristics as charity and forgiveness, my students would pick up these actions (or lack of them) as the example they should follow. Words are hollow to students, but actions demonstrate the sincerity of one's conviction.

John Locke writes, "I have always thought the actions of men the best interpreters of their thoughts." Students can attest to this well-known saying, "Too many churchgoers are singing 'Standing on the Promises' while they are just sitting on the premises." James said: "Be doers of the Word, and not hearers only." He explained that talk is cheap, but action costly as he wrote, "Religion that is pure and undefiled before God and the Father is this: to visit orphans and widows in their affliction, and to keep oneself unstained from the world" (1:22, 27).

Sunday school personnel are object lessons! They have a story to tell by their actions and attitudes. They can be objects of love *for* love in their ministry of teaching, or they can be objects as hollow as a balloon and as equally full of hot air.

There is a difficulty in being a teacher, but there is also much personal satisfaction in knowing that Christ working in and through you has made a lasting impression upon a student.

This is a lesson no Christian teacher should object to, but should respect!

Diploma to Discipleship

He disciplines us for our good, that we may share his holiness.
Heb. 12:10

We don't graduate from Sunday school, but there are annual promotions!

It's not recorded in Scripture that St. Paul marched to the strains of "Pomp and Circumstance" to receive his diploma in discipleship. Nor did he receive a degree following the blinding encounter with Jesus on the Damascus Road and his days of spiritual growth in that city. Nowhere do we read that the Twelve graduated with honors following their three-year course of instruction under the tutelage of Rabbi Jesus. There was no formal commencement; they simply commenced to *do* and *be* what the Lord had taught them.

As there were no ornamented, elaborated sheepskins awarded, no doctoral hoods, no accolades for performance or letter sweaters or trophies, so there were no pins or buttons or attendance awards either. Their diploma to discipleship was sharing in the holiness of the Triune God, in knowing personally and intimately Jesus Christ.

One cannot remove the idea of "discipline" from the concept of "discipleship." It is the almighty God who disciplines us through His Word, through life's experiences, to be truly His disciples. In the process, Christians share in His holiness, sanctified by His grace, hallowed by His love.

Fields of learning are referred to as disciplines, for each requires something of the student, yet none imparts as much joy as the discipline of faith. Corrected, redirected, instructed anew, Christians are disciplined for their own betterment by the caring Spirit.

In the parish's educational program for children there is a tendency to concentrate on details and techniques, on curriculum and facilities, when it is disciplining youth to be disciples that should command our most serious attention in the classroom.

Yes, punch-outs, coloring, flannelgraphs, and modeling clay are fun crafts that teach vital truths when we don't become so wrapped up in their technique that we forget to teach. "Give them some crayons and a piece of paper and that will keep them busy," suggested one well-meaning, but wrongly motivated Sunday school staff member.

The diploma to discipleship is never achieved through busywork—only through the work of *being* what Jesus teaches us we can and should be.

Extracurricular Activities

To the man who pleases him God gives wisdom and knowledge and joy; but to the sinner he gives the work of gathering and heaping, only to give to one who pleases God. This also is vanity and a striving after wind.
Eccl. 2:26

Name your sport, list your hobby, state your favorite pastime. Chances are, if Christ has a part in it, it is all the more enjoyable. Your job, your profession, your calling may be utter drudgery or complete ecstasy. The man in Christ knows the difference. He has discovered that both curricular and extracurricular activities have more meaning for the one who has answered God's call to serve.

It's not merely the income, the fringe benefits, the title.

It's the satisfaction, the pleasure, the joy that comes from teaming up with God to do His bidding. To distinguish between the enjoyment of activities on the job and on one's own time is nearly impossible. Both are to be enjoyed.

One man sees his profession as a job, another sees it as a contribution. One man recognizes his role is confining; another sees the same position as a continual challenge. It makes a difference with whom you counsel on such day-to-day matters as work and pleasure. When you confront the Spirit, you encounter happiness. For others life is merely "striving after wind."

Teachers need a break in their routine, as do students. But that "break" should be in their activity, not their foundation. Said an American clergyman of the last century, "Since I began to ask God's blessing on my students, I have done more in one week than I have done in a whole year before." Add to that prayer petitions on other activities, and the petitioner will discover more enjoyment bound up in limited opportunities than previously experienced in more significant ones.

Christians in education must learn that all of life belongs to God rather than one or two segments of it. In the process God is pleased, and the faithful rejoice.

Between Parson and Guile

So put away all malice and all guile and insincerity and envy and all slander.
1 Peter 2:1

Trapped between the two extremes of the ideal and the real, we often give in to the lesser one. Not that pastors are perfect; they're not, yet they represent the perfection of Christ, as should every Christian. There is the temptation, however, to think the clergy a little closer to perfection than others, a sad and unfortunate assumption. It is possible for any Christian who feels the pressures of life grinding away within to give in to craftiness and cunning, to guile and malice.

The tension between good and evil is an age-old plight. Ask Adam and Eve! Check it out with Cain! Inquire of Ananias and Sapphira! See what Peter and Thomas say about it, what Judas and Paul have to tell us!

Staff members are expected to lead exemplary lives. They are to be examples to students and the rest of the congregation. The problem is that perfection belongs to Christ, and striving to be like Him does not guarantee success. Failure is often the grade, for the exams are based on life situations.

A feeling of defeat is the result of a deadly legalism which knows no forgiveness, applies little love, and refuses to recognize man's imperfect ability to think. By contrast, God loves the sinner while hating the sin. He knows how to separate the wheat from the chaff, to find the kernel of truth, and to gain from it the healthy nutrient. Surely this is a trait we do well to cultivate, so that we can find in every mistake a lesson for the future, in every unpleasantness a hope for change, and the understanding and patience that God gives us through His love.

When caught between the parson and guile, remember one is a human being and the other a human emotion. Human beings can understand. When pressures plague you, your pastor will be more helpful than what you can expect from deceit and cunning.

A Schoolhouse of Trees

(Zacchaeus) sought to see who Jesus was, but could not, on account of the crowd, because he was small of stature. So he ran on ahead and climbed up into a sycamore tree to see him, for he was to pass that way.
Luke 19:3-4

Zacchaeus didn't expect an education. All he wanted was to see this man named Jesus that he had heard the marketplace buzzing about. His tree became a schoolroom, and he learned more from that experience than he had the rest of his life.

A new mission congregation was fortunate to use the lovely chapel of a nearby graduate school, but there were insufficient classrooms for the Sunday school and their adult program called "The Institute for Christian Growth," a name they shortened to "In+Christ+Grow." The only alternative was to use the lovely lawn about the Tell Interfaith Center in the Arizona suburb of Phoenix called Glendale. Each class had its own tree.

Only Arizonans know how fortunate having a tree is. There are few towering trees in the desert. Only where irrigation has been used and imported trees planted will you find the tall shade trees that are commonplace in the Midwest. The mild winter temperatures made the trees ideal most of the cool season, but they didn't provide sufficient insulation in the steamy heat of August. Every tree on that shade-dusted lawn was a Zacchaean classroom.

Children and adults alike were learning what that little man of Jericho discovered: When Christ has your attention, every place is a learning center.

The disciples knew that. Jesus instructed them with the visual aids of fig trees and fields of grain. He made the supper table a classroom. Hiking from place to place became more than a nature study; it became a study of the nature of love, the love that recognized the faith of little children, and the aching needs of a thieving tax collector like Zacchaeus.

There was another who learned from trees. It was the blind man of Bethsaida, who felt Jesus' healing touch and looked up, saying, "I see men; but they look like trees walking." A second time Jesus touched him, and he "saw everything clearly" (Mark 8:22ff).

It was the tree of the cross that became a schoolhouse for all of us. And we continue learning from it.

Imaginative Evangelism

But new wine must be put into fresh wineskins.
Luke 5:38

There are some who opt for the old ways of teaching.

There are others who seek new methods, avant-garde techniques, fresh ideas!

The wisdom of Scripture points out that new wine requires brand new wineskins, lest the old swell under the fermentation of the new batch, beyond their capacity. "And no one after drinking old wine desires new; for he says, 'The old is better' " (Luke 5:39). Jesus provided a fitting conclusion to his observation.

Whether or not it is true of education is something He leaves us to judge, but surely we may make several assumptions.

1. New ideas need testing in fresh young lives.

2. Old methods may be as exciting today as in the past, if the instructor has the enthusiasm and the certain conviction that the techniques are invaluable.

3. Whether "new wine" or "old," the objective is to produce first-rate wine, which can neither be a hurried-up matter or one in which concern for the objective is not assured.

When it comes to children in Sunday school or the Christian

34

day school, we do well to clarify our goals before we start making wine. Soda pop may be nice, but it's hardly wine. Mouthwash may be helpful, but it can't replace wine. Aged wine requires one kind of method, while new wine demands another.

One Sunday school superintendent saw attendance decline sharply in her primary department. It was easy to blame "birth control" and watch the downward slide go even further. She wasn't that easily derailed from her objective of reaching the community's children for Christ.

Apartment houses had risen in the neighborhood, and many children were to be found there. Many came from different cultural backgrounds than the founders of the congregation. The old pattern of doing things needed new life, and she brainstormed with her staff about ways that might be helpful.

There was the old method of door-to-door evangelism. They put new life into it by giving each child they met a balloon with an invitation tied to it. They released hundreds of helium-filled balloons in the area with the same message, and the resulting publicity stimulated interest.

Meanwhile, the staff determined to put away their flannelgraphs for a time and set aside the filmstrip projector. They turned their primary-department room into a three-dimensional setting for the lesson of the day. When it was about Noah, they arranged their benches like an ark in which the children crawled as symbolic animals. When they learned about the Garden of Eden, the room was filled with potted plants. When they shared the story of the Good Samaritan, the teachers acted out the parts in costume, and the children repeated it adding their own interpretation.

It was amazingly successful. There was nothing startlingly new. There was fresh enthusiasm and the assurance their objective was being more successfully fulfilled.

If new wine requires fresh wineskins, be assured the old wineskins may still have a purpose, and the vintage may be more savory than ever.

Child Talk

When I was a child, I spoke like a child, I thought like a child, I reasoned like a child.
1 Cor. 13:11

Eric is a bright-haired, large-eyed three-year-old. He isn't always enthusiastic about attending worship services, because sitting still is not as much fun as his youthful mind can dream of. But there is a part of the service he likes.

It's the pastor's "Black Bag," a small flight bag in which the pastor hides all manner of things he uses in his object-lesson sermonettes for the children. Sometimes he has had candy there. Once it was pretzels. Another time it was a seashell, and still another it was a large desert tortoise who fit snugly in the bottom of the "Black Bag."

One Sunday the Pastor decided to omit the object lesson. It seemed children felt awkward about coming forward, and he thought they had lost interest. He was going to shelve it, but Eric changed the plans abruptly.

"Well," said the three-year-old to his mother, "if God isn't going to have the 'Black Bag' anymore, I'm not coming to church." It was cut and dried. He had been left out, and his resentment was readily understood by others.

He was told that God hadn't decided to leave the object lesson out. That was the pastor's doing, but it would be quickly reinstated the following week. And it was. And it probably will never be abandoned again.

Children say some pretty colorful things. Many times they penetrate decorum and puncture smugness.

Eric was right to demand his part in the worship service, just as other youngsters have a right to demand a part in the classroom, at home, in Sunday school. When they are deprived of a role of their own, you can count on their showing their resentment in one way or another. Sometimes the clue is found in youthful indignation as voiced by Eric. Other times it's by out-and-out rebellion. Between these extremes there exist many variables, but inevitably the observant teacher will discover that somewhere along the line the youngster was overlooked. His or her needs were considered unimportant.

Jesus was first to single out the child and to meet its needs with sensitivity.

Popcorn Paraments

And a little child shall lead them
Is. 11:6

There is a young, thriving congregation in Tempe, Arizona, that recognizes the talents of everyone. When they began their mission several years ago, it was suggested that all of their chancel furnishings should be made by members. None of it had to have permanence. It could be used only one week or for a month; but whatever it would be, it would come from the hands, hearts, and faith of the people.

That included children.

In their Sunday school classes they made colorful paraments of paper for the altar and pulpit. Unlike the costly silk brocades of most churches, these simple works of art were not valuable in terms of money, but what they expressed provided worshipers with a wealth of inspiration.

How about paraments of strung popcorn, or cross and candlesticks of carved styrofoam, or pastoral vestments of crayoned flowers, or banners of chain-linked construction paper?

37

Why not let the children grow their flowers for the altar, or make them of pipe cleaners?

For some this involvement of the people may remove some of the stately beauty of the chancel. That may not be altogether bad. But the expressions of young and old, brilliant and mentally retarded, gifted and ordinary may add a personal dimension that gives life to the chancel and joy to the contributor. We cannot all give jewel-encrusted chalices or expensive polished-brass altarware, but we can use the talents God has given us to make His house a chamber festival that emulates the Lord Jesus who wanted all children brought to Him. "And forbid them not," He said, "for of such is the kingdom of God."

Sunday school classes may become temporary altar guilds, fashioning new symbols for ancient Biblical truths, or taking the well-known symbols of the past and adding an interpretation that may far more effectively relate the Gospel to today.

God has endowed children with vivid imaginations. They are a wonderful resource for congregational renewal. They are an asset that needs being put to work.

Too Many Hats?

One thing is needful.
Luke 10:42

When a Christian gets involved in the life of his church and community, he sometimes discovers that he has more hats than headroom. It seems impossible to keep up with all the meetings, all the responsibilities, as well as all the preparation that each new assignment requires.

When Martha found herself overbusy and distracted by her

chores as a housekeeper and hostess, Jesus told her, "One thing is needful."

Caring for her soul was more important than all the other duties she could conjure up, from dusting to dishwashing.

The marvel, however, is that when a person takes action to fortify his soul, he discovers more than ample energy and time to tackle the various duties before him. Frustration comes from concentrating more on the hats than the head.

And the heart!

Take Jesus as an example. No one was more badgered by outsiders wanting a special interview than He was. When the sick learned He was near, they jammed the roadway. When the spiritually unfilled listened to His sermons, they virtually backed Him into the sea. His disciples tried to chase away noisy children and their mothers, but Jesus wanted to see them and scolded the thoughtful Twelve for preventing such precious ones from entering into His presence, tired or not. The secret was that Jesus took time out for prayer. There were no quickies. Prayer wasn't a hurried-up process.

When we get our head straight spiritually and our hearts beating in rhythm to the Word and will of God, we can wear more hats than we thought possible.

Frustration takes a back seat. Weariness flies out the window. "Poor me" and other "games" disappear.

Why Venice has stagnant canals, I'm not sure, but the reason Amsterdam remains fairly clean is that they flush out the canals every night by leaving only one gate to the sea open. During the day, canal traffic requires nearly every entry to be open. But the nightly cleansing is still necessary. For Christians, too, "one thing is needful." Regular spiritual cleansing purifies and energizes a Christian's life.

Professionalism

Encourage one another and build one another up, just as you are doing.
1 Thess. 5:11

Professionalism is a highly regarded quality among medical people, journalists, and educators, as well as others. Sometimes it means a kind of hard polish that will not yield to irritants. Perhaps it is better known as pride.

Pride can surely be devastatingly destructive. It can prove arrogant and defiant, smug and confident. But that isn't professionalism at its best or pride as God would have it.

There is pride in the ranks of church school workers oftentimes. Much of it is wholesome, but every now and then it becomes a devilish technique that seeks to destroy the school's ministry. More experienced workers may be jealous of their less experienced, but more popular colleagues. Oldtimers may have experiences to share that newcomers would benefit by, but refuse.

Professionalism in the Sunday school means a genuine concern that the staff professes what the school intends to proclaim. If love is part of that proclamation, then jealousy has no place. If forgiveness is part of it, then hurt feelings and gossip and sharp tongues have to be dealt with forgivingly. If fulfilling the Great Commission is included in that proclamation, then gaining every insight into improved teaching techniques is vitally important.

That goes one step further. Professionalism in the church school demands a mutuality of purpose and a corporate concern that is underscored by each staff member encouraging the others, complimenting their achievements, and offering help to face difficulties together. If one instructor has a problem, it belongs to the whole staff. If one student is troubled, the concern is shared by all on the faculty. Together, in prayer and action, through supportive effort and humble co-laboring, problems are confronted with positive hope, and the troubled know the measure of love is more than word deep.

Professionalism is professing the Gospel by living it rather than just talking about it. That's why the disciples succeeded in turning the world upside down for Jesus.

Vacations

The Lord watches over the sojourners.
Psalms 146:9

Who has more holidays, more vacation periods, than the students—unless it is those who teach?

Frequently instructors spend their time off grading papers, taking courses, attending seminars, which is part and parcel of the professional who keeps abreast of what's happening, the new ideas upcoming, and explores new fields.

The comforting fact is that these moments away from the classroom are blessings of God. The student plays hard or works aggressively during these respites from learning. The faculty member rests, takes care of household chores, and fills the time with other professional duties. Yet these minutes are under the provisions of the Almighty.

Scattered in every direction when school lets out for summer, the student body and instructors head for beaches and mountains, tours abroad, and vacation jobs at home. These varied activities are not without notice to the Triune God, who makes them a refreshing blessing, a time of renewal and strengthening.

A student is ready once again to dig into books.

A teacher is happy to return to the classroom and share the new understandings gained throughout the summer months.

May it be, however, that both those who teach and those who learn will not forget each other, but frequently seek Divine blessings upon the other. May it be that whatever has been learned will be applied to life and tested. Pope has reasoned, "There is no study that is not capable of delighting us after a little application to it."

Welcome vacations as the God-given chance to put truth into action and enjoy the results.

School Cheer

As the truth of Christ is in me, this boast of mine shall not be silenced.
2 Cor. 11:10

"Clap your hands, all peoples! Shout to God with loud songs of joy!" The psalmist was a cheerleader of sorts. He frequently called to the believers to express their loyalty to God in shouts of jubilation, in rhythmic applause, and in songs of praise.

Each Christian is called upon to be one of God's cheerleaders, urging the timid to express their joy, and the faithful to exult in Christ.

Perhaps there are no distinctive uniforms, unless it be the one Paul calls for us to put on in Ephesians 6:10ff, but surely the colors of faith are flown 24 hours a day by the Christian who has the King in residence within his heart.

We need to cheer on the teams that are struggling to win victories to the glory of God, that are less upon the gridiron and more within the Church. We need to encourage youth to stand up and shout their loyalty to Christ. We need to work on the "alumni," those delinquent church members whose loyalty is slipping into oblivion. We need to inspire the faculty to sing not only the Alma Mater but the songs of faith. And the coaches, those leaders within parishes and schools, communities and organizations that endeavor to better our lot, them too we need to cheer by the encouragement of prayer.

And of what shall we boast?

Our expertise in basketball, our superior scholarship, our allegiance to a thorough list of rules? No!

Let our boast be in Christ, and our cheers will be magnified by the thousands who join with us in more than a local school yell, by the cheers that belong to all who are studying within the School of Christian Faith.

And perhaps that shout will be no more than "Hallelujah!"

But that's the Bible's cheer for God, and one we should have no trouble exclaiming.

Detention

God is treating you as sons; for what son is there whom his father does not discipline? If you are left without discipline, in which all have participated, then you are illegitimate children and not sons. Hebrews 12:7-8

There was no need for Jesus to keep any of His students after school. They may not always have pleased Him, but their purpose for following Him about, for absorbing His message with eagerness, and doing what they were instructed—from ministering to virtual outcasts to trampling across Galilee, through Samaria, to Judea—was simply to be His disciples. Disciplined for action, they were not anxious to begin the task the Lord gave them at His

Ascension, but when the Holy Spirit came they moved out into the world, fully trained, to share the Gospel.

Being detained after school or before classes begin in the morning is not pleasant for student or teacher, yet it's frequently necessary if the student is to learn something more than a few facts. Love has to be the reason, but even love may be experienced in stern words and actions of discipline.

Acknowledged educator John Dewey, "Discipline means power at command; mastery of the resources available for carrying through the actions undertaken. To know what one is to do and to move to do it promptly and by the use of the requisite means is to be disciplined, whether we are thinking of an army or the mind. Discipline is positive."

A student balked at being required to remain after class. "What for?" he wanted to know.

The instructor's wave of the forefinger instructed him to be seated, and then the teacher began to speak. "I have often had to ask you to remain after school, Chris," he said. "You have often been disruptive and inattentive, but I want you to know that today your participation in class, your mannerliness, and eagerness to contribute have made this one of the best days I have had. Thank you." Detention paid off; discipline was rewarded.

The Big Game

Do you not know that in a race all the runners compete, but only one receives the prize? So run that you may obtain it. Every athlete exercises self-control in all things. They do it to receive a perishable wreath, but we an imperishable. Well, I do not run aimlessly, I do not box as one beating the air; but I pommel my body and subdue it, lest after preaching to others I myself should be disqualified.
1 Cor. 9:24-27

The players exercised to the cadence called by their coach. They made the required laps with almost breathless speed. They were in training for the **BIG GAME!** It was the chief contest of the season, and each man was polishing his technique to assure another victory.

The cheer leaders were practicing their latest yells, and the band was warming up to the spirit of the event. Posters and handbills called upon the student body to support the eager team at the forthcoming rally and the subsequent game. There was a determined and positive attitude being molded by the coaching staff, and the athletes readily responded.

Christianity is always in training, and it recognizes every struggle to be the **BIG GAME** at that moment. Coached by Scripture, disciplined by the Sacraments, trained in the arenas of life itself, Christians find themselves equipped to win, only to discover that it's possible to falter if cockiness or disenchantment is allowed to transform positive certainty into negative confusion. It can be like the old gag about the contest at the coliseum: Lions 100; Christians 0!

Student athletes fight on two battlefronts. They must be in good condition physically as well as academically. Instructors have a double front line also in continuing education as well as

45

teaching. Christians know that readiness for combat, whether intellectual or moral, is required always. There is no such thing as readying oneself but once. To win means to keep in shape in every discipline.

Are you spending time well training in the arena of prayer? Are you exercising your spiritual muscle frequently by a constant, steady, faithful witness? Are you ready for today's BIG GAME?

BMOC

Whoever exalts himself will be humbled, and whoever humbles himself will be exalted.
Matt. 23:12

The nostalgic revival of styles and customs of the fifties brings to mind that title often given to a popular guy, BMOC, "Big Man on Campus." He may have excelled in campus politics or athletics. He may have come from a prominent family or achieved a high academic award. He was still BMOC.

It was easily seen that many of these lads had feet of clay. They were not omnipotent, although their rivals frequently thought they were omnipresent. Their popularity was not easily squelched, albeit detractors certainly tried. If they were not BMOC to everyone, they still maintained their close-knit coterie of friends. To them they were invincible, that is, until they stumbled over their feet of clay.

It was often thought that such BMOC would be crowned homecoming king, and their female counterpart named queen, but somehow the majority always chose the less flashy candidate for the title. The choice was Biblically sound. The exalted were humbled, and the humbled raised up to places of honor.

Self-confidence can never be merely conceit. Knowledge does

not equate with arrogance. Popularity does not guarantee substance. Thus BMOC's are knocked off their pedestals by perceptive colleagues who look for more than superficial beauty. The BMOC too often cares only for himself, whereas the humble instructor, the thoughtful student may put all others first. Such qualities may go unnoticed seemingly, but not for long. And when humility is exercised sincerely rather than mockingly, God knows and God elevates.

Pride can be a useful tool, but it may also become self-defeating. Within the academic circle there is no better example after which to pattern one's ego and life than that of Jesus, who was certain of where He was headed, but unafraid to take the servant's role. Now that's a genuine Big Man on Campus.